50p
15

Small things
that
MATTER

D1634660

William Ayot

THE WELL AT
OLIVIER MYTHODRAMA PUBLISHING

First published 2003 by
The Well at Olivier Mythodrama Publishing

Olivier Mythodrama Associates Ltd
PO Box 44165
London
SW6 6TL
books@oma.uk.com
www.oliviermythodrama.com

Cover illustration from a watercolour by Jenny Barron
in the author's collection.

Typeset in Janson. Designed by Firstproof.
Printed in Great Britain by Print Forum.

For the grandfathers

and

for Juliet

Contents

I

ECHOES AND VOICES

A Poem that Speaks for Itself

I am not a piece to be left on the page,
to be flicked over, licked at and spat out by the eye.
I am not to be read on the way to something else.
I take time. I'm a poem. I was made to be spoken.

I hold the sounds that connect you to the world,
the clicks and the splats and the crunches of life.
In me you can hear the song of the nightingale,
the yell of the vixen and the boom of distant waves.

When you speak me, when you utter me,
note the home of your voice: where it settles,
where it lives, what part of you it inhabits.
Now move on, explore the geography of vowels;
place an '*ee*' in your head, an '*ah*' in your chest.
Sense the well of emotion below every sound.
Next, take a careful quantity of consonants.
Mix them with the vowels. Add meaning to feeling.
Say, *hurt*. Say, *desire*. Say, *beauty*. Say, *loss*.
Say, *the woods are empty*. Say, *I long to belong*.

Now you know the form, you can improvise,
become a curlew, or a monkey, or a blue guitar.
You can free the music, conjure up some fun,
make the madness yours, let the laughter flow.
Above all, you can let the silence in me speak.
Don't be afraid... Let it hold what it will.

When you finally get to the foot of the page,
you can put me down and walk away.
Until then, I want you to speak every syllable,
to embrace every solitary, sensual word.
I may be no more than another page of poetry,
but when you recite me, we both come alive.

Speaking for Cinna

Shakespeare's Globe, September 1999

Four hundred years ago today, they came
to the Globe, our ancestors of blood and speech.
They came from Cheapside and Poultry, Ludgate
and St Botolph's, from Newington Causeway
to London Bridge, and through the muddy lanes.
They came for the usual stew of reasons:
for fellowship, laughter, learning and escape,
for excitement, for tears, and maybe to meet
a pair of eyes, within the wooden O.
They came to hear a play...
                                        high tragedy,
Shakespeare's *'Tragedie of Julius Caesar'.*
Pole-star-Caesar, fixed and brought down.
There was pride and resentment, honour
and the lack of it, but most of all
there was oratory, crystal oratory:
the word as power, as leash, as lash.
My blood remembers the excitement,
the ecstasy in which I was swayed.
But something in me still palls and shudders
when I think of the death of Cinna the poet;
cornered, reduced to five petty words.
I am Cinna the poet. I am Cinna the poet.

When terror comes the poets die first:
the romantics, the fools, the sayers of sooth.
Shakespeare got it right, he always got it right.
He knew that eloquence overwhelms truth,
that poetry is precious but also fragile.

Four hundred years – we've lost a lot of poets –
and our politics have created a clever world.
I think of Osip Mandelstam, dying
on his way to the Gulag, of the great
Akhmatova outside one of Stalin's jails.
I think of Frederico Garcia Lorca
meeting the eyes of the firing squad.
And I think of poets who never had a name,
whose words never flew from the printed page,
poets from Chile, Paraguay and China
who died unheard, in the terrible silence.

Today, with war reduced to a business,
and eloquence to the sound-bite and the clip,
we have come again to form a circle,
to see and maybe still to hear this play.
Four hundred years later I speak for Cinna
and the truths that are endangered today.
We live in a world that is shallow and glib.
I charge you, conjure you – no, I beg you.
Remember Cinna. Listen to your poets.

Christ Church, Spitalfields

For Nigel North

The music talks to the architecture
and the exhausted church leans in to listen,
pillars soaring high into the emptiness,
still rising, as all things once rose up.
The lute is plaintive, each note a beseechment,
and the attendant silence grows heavy
with the weight of gradual darkening –
prelude, allemande, courante, sarabande.

This is the baroque, the art of the vertical,
where all things ascend, where God
is the sky at the top of a chimney, where
there's nowhere you'd want to look but up.
Drawn to the light, we tore down the chimneys,
gleefully blasted the dull and limiting stacks.
What we found was a vast and beckoning horizon.
What we lost was a ready stairway to God.
In the broad light the sacred has lost its magic
and with it the power to comfort or curb.
A flat and well-meant list of platitudes
now havers in place of awe and wonderment.
Who remembers to hallow or to laud,
or notes that all things have their season?
Who cares for the stories that shaped a world,
that spoke of comfort, healing and grace?

Sarabande to gavotte and gavotte to gigue –
as Shakespeare followed tragedy with absurdity
so Bach leads us up and out of slow despair.
The last notes dwindle into nothingness
and we are left with the rubble of an age,
a memory of music and a silent, empty temple.
How hollow we are. How little we give.
In the silence you can sense the yearning.

Anyone Can Sing

Anyone can sing. You just open your mouth
and give shape to a sound. Anyone can sing.
What is harder is to proclaim the soul,
to initiate a wild and necessary deepening:
to give the voice broad, sonorous wings
of solitude, grief, and celebration,
to fill the body with the echoes of voices
lost long ago to bravery, and silence,
to prise the reluctant heart wide open,
to witness defeat, to suffer contempt,
to shrink, lose face, go down in ignominy,
to retreat to the last dark hiding-place
where the tattered remnants of your pride
still gather themselves around your nakedness,
to know these rags as your only protection
and yet still open – to face the possibility
that your innermost core may hold nothing at all,
and to sing from that – to fill the void
with every hurt, every harm, every hard-won joy
that staves off death yet honours its coming,
to sing both full and utterly empty,
alone and conjoined, exiled and at home,
to sing what people feel most keenly
yet never acknowledge until you sing it.
Anyone can sing. Yes. Anyone can sing.

II

THE GRIEF BETWEEN US

Rain

Rain this morning, and the house surrendering,
settling in random plops and splashes. Outside
my window an elder tree is coming into leaf.
I recall the thick summer scent of elder, the rich
autumnal heaviness of the berries, pea-shooters
made out of hollow stems.
                                                Darker thoughts too,
about the witch-tree, brooding by the cottage door.
Ancient village grudges settled with a cruelty.
Puritan good-wives pointing the spiteful finger,
widow-women, named and burned on the green.

And then my mother, unhinged by widowhood,
palsied with fear and clinging like a five year old.
Tried and damned in her own relentless witch hunt,
but the burning bungled and the corpse left alive.

Maybe I'll just listen to the rain this morning,
making its shapeless music round the house.
Maybe I'll wait and then head for the hospital.
It'll all be over soon enough – all be over soon.

The Gift Refused

No one can hurt me the way you hurt me
with a sloppy word or a gift refused.
No one but you can wield the twisted wand
of enchantment and abandonment
so ruthlessly, so thoughtlessly.
A casual remark and I am your boy again,
the pair of us pinned in the family album,
longing and loathing and saying we mean it.
Or you, years later, beyond all knowing,
with your hormones shot after the operation,
instinctively pushing me away in disgust
when I finally thought you might want me
to hold you.
                    Easier to say no in the light
of such a learning, easier to stop chasing
the notion of a love that maybe never existed.
Yet here I am in the gloom of Intensive Care,
keeping watch like the father over the way,
waiting by the shell of his only daughter.
Humming a lullaby, hoping against hope.

The Edge

My mother lies in the High Dependency Unit,
serene and comfortable as a corpse.
The machinery is muttering an antiphon
as she sleeps off the effects of the temazepam.

I watch her sunken, disendentured face.
She is oddly beautiful, an alabaster abbess
laid out calmly on a crisp white monument.

Part of me wants it to be over.

Slow heart, says the staff-nurse, beaming
at the monitor which seems to float above us.
There's the busy sound of a stomach pump,
and retching from over the way.
                                    That's it...
she says cheerily, diving through a curtain.
Lovely. That's the spirit. Better out than in.

My mother wakes and struggles to focus.
She smiles. There's a little edge of triumph.
You came, she whispers. *I knew you would.*
You were always the first to come to me.

Confessional

Three days after doing the deed
she's still marooned in the H.D.U.,
compos now and on the mend, but sheepish,
thoughtful, aware of the damage she's done
to herself and the delicate lace of her relationships.
My anger, abating for want of somewhere to put it,
has given way to a dull and dogged patience,
to the bland bonhomie of the regular visitor.
I listen as she talks through the last few days,
saving and sorting, picking through the oddments.
She grows quiet. She shrinks. I ask what's going on.
I wanted to die, she whispers. *I let him down.*

Tumbled Statues

Small things matter now: the kiss, the smile,
the stroking of her face, the fat tear
falling as I eat my failure
to save or salve or halt the clock.
I am the parent now and she the child,
escaping to places where she is held
by the harsh enchantments of the past.
We sit in silence. There are no more words.
We are tumbled statues, our heads leant together
by some upheaval deep within the earth.
Inches from mine her eyelids flutter open,
the red-raw tear ducts like wounds
in the parchment skin. I whisper a welcome
and her dull eyes fill with present pain.
My mother, returning from another world.

Dasht-I-Margo

There's grief between us now,
and what they call the disintegration of the self,
the long cold desert that dries out thoughts,
that leaves them parched, and bleached
and finally eroded.
                      Nothing meets nothing
on the high plateau, except that now and again
she looks at me as if I were a stranger,
an Afghan tribesman, wrapped in misty grey,
appearing out of nowhere in the Dasht-I-Margo.
Seen through the glass of her imaginings,
I loom like a brigand in her Desert-of-Death.
She flinches. I withdraw but it's too late.
Her loathing cuts me like a knife.

The Scarlet Woman

A good day is when she lifts her head,
when we sit in a clearing of tenderness.
In the calm she makes little animal noises,
half-sighs and pipings, the beginnings of a laugh.
Other days she takes my hand and looks at it,
tries to say something, then dips into shame.

It's the shame that harrows: the chin on the chest,
the tiny voice that responds to the nurses;
the gulp, the swallow, the offering of her neck,
the willing of a punishment she's made her own.

Add fear and brimstone to a world of shame
and the life of a lonely old woman can harden
to create a self-hating purgatory:
the neighbours who spat at her for living in sin,
the rector who refused to bless her marriage,
the brazen turning away from the church,
the wistful Sundays spent listening to hymns
that thundered from the Bakelite radio.
All reduced to a pair of trembling hands,
wringing out the voices, unable to pray.

He Talks to His Mother of Troubadours

Weedy little geezer, there's nothing of him.
Torn leather jacket, grubby jeans and sneakers,
a broken-down guitar that's seen better days.
He's a busker, an illegal, a latter-day Blondin
singing to commuters on the Underground.
He's got it down to a fine art – timing
his songs between Northern Line trains –
one eye on the indicator, the other peeled
for the police. A three-minute song
and then a rattle along the platform,
smiling his thanks to suburban rejection.

Spare a little change for the song, My Lady?

Every night it's the same old gig: '*American Pie*'
and '*San Francisco*', sung between trains
for Edgware or Barnet or Mill Hill East.

And then one night he sang something different,
fierce and melancholy, moorish and strange.
The station was empty. The platform was deserted,
and he sang as if to fill the spaces
with the breadth of his soul, as a kind of thank you.
It was raw and ecstatic, breaking free
of the words, and I was held by ancestral voices
from Africa and Asia, Toulouse and Montsegur,
keening the long diaspora of song.

I put my hand in my pocket but he had vanished.

The next night it was back to '*American Pie*',
to ducking and diving and avoiding the uniforms,
grinning and smiling as the punters ignored him.

Spare some change to feed the song, Lady?
Spare a bit of silver to keep the song alive?

. . .

I wish you could see him, Mother.
I wish you could get up out of your plastic chair,
throw your happy-pills in the sink,
and walk right out of that psycho-ward.
I wish you could walk down into the Underground,
and join the people you were always so scared of.
I wish you could listen to this funny little man
with his pitiful repertoire and his rattling tin
because I think he might help you, Mother,
not with the magic of his voice or inheritance
but with his persistence in the face of indifference.
As I sat with you tonight I heard him singing
twenty-five miles down the line.
The words of his song were swirling around us –

You love, and you suffer, and you carry on.

III

OTHER DEMANDS

Another Kind of High

It's a different kind of buzz, a body-high,
your own raw chemicals pumping madly
like you've just jumped out of a plane.
The ivorine roulette-ball clatters like a rattle
and cards leave the dealer's hands like birds.
You can feel the breeze of them passing you,
fluttering; and all the time you're falling
into space, free as a diver or a mountaineer,
falling.
          The winning means nothing to you
when you're addicted, falling into the void.
What is real is the ground-rush and the flat,
unholy glow you get when you finally hit
the deck – smack, busted, not a penny left,
no credit, no change, you've done the lot.
It isn't the excitement that gets to a gambler.
The high for him is leaving broke – soaked
and sated, wrung-out, empty.
                              You can see it
when they say good-night, it's in their rueful
four o'clock smiles. They've hit the ground
but they're still falling...

The Gambler's Prayer

The casino is empty, like a pharaoh's tomb,
but the man at the end of my black jack table
is hanging on in there, wanking away a fiver.
He no longer smiles when he calls for a card,
just taps the table with a trembling finger,
and at every shuffle he looks up, baffled,
his red eyes full of the usual questions:
How could this happen? What do I tell them?
Where can I go to get another hundred?
You don't need to know him to have him pegged.
He's a quiet man, kindly, good with the kids,
probably never been unfaithful in his life.
But he gambles, swings out over the emptiness,
night after night, enchanted, enthralled.
                                        I call
last hand but he hardly notices. He's too busy
mumbling the gambler's prayer: *Lord, let me*
break even tonight. I really need the money.

A Silence

My father is nursing a glass of India Pale Ale
while my mother is wiping down the bar,
hanging damp tea-towels over the pumps.
I'm sitting in the inglenook, feet against the fire,
gripping a book entitled '*Disasters For Boys*',
and wishing I hadn't come in for lunch.
Something has been said, some wounding truth,
about money or love or the lack of both.
My father has taken it on the chin, he's reeling,
while my mother has a frozen look about her,
a blend of defiance and appalled realisation.
She's gazing down at her work-scarred hands
as if they were holding a smoking revolver.
My dad looks down at the rich, chestnut beer,
hoping for a kindness or a sudden inspiration.
I look down too, because that's what we do
in our diffident, demoralised, defeated clan.
There's a faint scent of beeswax on my fingers
and the musty library smell of the book.
The logs stop their spitting and, outside the window,
the sparrows give up their incessant bickering.
My mother stays scared. My father stays empty
and I am learning to stay invisible. In the silence
our sad, exhausted family is scattered to the winds.

The Volunteer's Tale

Sometimes we fail. They go back on the street.
You're supposed to shrug and be professional,
say it was their choice, and philosophise
about process or the endless cycles of karma.
I can't do that. I'd make a lousy therapist.
Part of me slopes off with them, you see:
confused and muttering, full of self-hatred,
half-expecting to die on the embankment,
freezing, or raving, or bleeding from the ears,
murdered for a bottle or a twenty-pound bag.
Spare a thought if not a blessing, for Patrick
Joseph Aloysious: crazy, cavalier, demanding Pat
whose cirrhotic liver left him smelling like a drain,
mocked by the women, despised by the men,
seen through by us all in his petty manipulations.
Patrick, who had done the most terrible things,
whose darkness spread out from him like a mist,
creeping, insinuating, unnerving, discomfiting,
his puffy red hands still slick with the horror
of acts you'd have to be drunk to imagine.
Paddy who, ten months into the programme,
discovered what it was that had made him drink:
the unholy memory of the Christian Brothers,
of the pillows his silent sobs were pushed into,
of the bodies and the breath and the poisonous lie.

A word of this, my son, and you will burn.

Spare a thought for Patrick Joseph Aloysious
who couldn't face the pain of getting a life,
who would rather die than re-visit his boyhood
and the feral scream that never leaves the body,
that hangs in the heart like a twisted crucifix,
leaving you filthy and tarnished, and numb.
Pat made his choice. He went back on the street.

And on the Seventh Day

God knows, it's easy enough to point the finger.
We're all churchwardens when we read the papers.
Disgust and self-righteousness are par for the course
on a slow suburban Sunday morning.

But at night,
when the tom-cats of loneliness call, and things
that live on secrets stretch themselves and stir.
Then dapper little accountants from Wimbledon
reach for the phone with a trembling hand
to whisper obscenities to part-time women
who yawn as they do it for them – do it all night.
Then salesmen, surveyors and warehousemen,
plasterers and clerks and the occasional priest,
the meek and the mild and the simply ordinary,
step into the neon-twisted light, blinking
and gulping and slowly transforming themselves
into leather-clad predators or hungry-angry lads.
Then the Chairman, the Chief, the public man,
waits in his car at the edge of the Common,
or walks among the silent, cruising shadows,
risking the world for a moment of excitement,
for a buzz that his daylight self can't allow.
And somewhere in the bushes, with his heart
in his mouth, stands a man whom we nod to
or smile at in the supermarket. And he's scared
and excited and feeling foolish, as he waits there,
naked but for a raincoat. And he's not too sure
why he's there again, or why the siren voices
should have brought him back.

But he's back
and he's driven to show himself to a woman
who may scream when she sees what he is doing,
or hurry by in shame, or call for the police.
And the rest of him will sit on Sunday morning,
flicking through the usual spread of crucifixions.
And once again he'll feel that little pang of envy
when he reads about the sinners who can rest.

Junkie Funeral

Seventeen strangers at a junkie funeral.
All of them on smack – not a feeling in sight,
just the slow, seeping sadness of a user's exit,
the farewells and the war stories –
like their parents only thinner.

He died alone, crashed-out in a corner.
Nobody noticed that he'd quietly slipped away.
So this morning they're celebrating,
the only way they know how –
making the usual calculations,
balancing their highs and trusting to luck –
some valium to take the fear out of the hash,
so much coke to lift the smack.

The talk turns to dealers and how
they used to be better. How they'd never stoop
to selling you second-rate gear.
And if they did, why, they'd always tell you.
It's crap, they'd say by way of an apology.
But I'll see you right. There's good stuff coming.

Meanwhile his widow practises numbness
while the baby gently tumbles inside her,
junked-up, strung-out before it's drawn a breath.
She looks at the coffin with something akin to envy
and smiles at the junkie who sold them their first fix.
Finally, she takes in her circle of strangers.
It's what he would have wanted, she says.

IV

SOMETHING
WE DRIVE THROUGH

井

Myxie

You follow the work. You sample the City
and soon enough the City seems like home.
The air gets thicker, things decay around you
and the sky is livid but you get used to it.
Then comes the day you try to remember
what a coot's egg looks like, and you can't,
or the smell of sorrel or docks or cow-parsley.
All you can remember is the myxie'd rabbit
you once saw, running doolally in a field,
the one with the suppurating eyes and mouth,
beating its head against a weatherboard fence.

Eggardon Hill

You slept, and while you slept I climbed the hill,
treading again the ancient winding path
that leads from the combe to the grass-grown fort,
leads to the silences born of the climb.

I brought you violets of different kinds
with primroses and yellow celandines
and something small and white I didn't know
that grew by a freshet that broke from the hill.

I brought you a blue-black raven's feather
and curiosities plucked from the turf,
a grinning root-ball, weathered like a skull,
snail-shells and wonders that caught the thin light.

I brought you shining multicoloured stones
that lay like jewels on the rain-slicked path
and a thorn-twig bearing a shred of wool
that smelled of lanolin and innocence.

On my return I made you a 'pies nest,
a circle of treasures, laid out to please:
flowers and stones in juxtaposition
that spoke of the view I'd wanted to share.

You slept, and waiting I watched over you
as the evening gathered and the pebbles dried,
the flowers withered and the wool blew away
leaving us nothing but thorns and a skull.

These two treasures I brought back from Eggardon,
natural keepsakes wrapped up in a view.
The view, the wind and the rain I'll remember,
but you, you slept...

Houseflies in February

Houseflies on my window-pane,
walking across the sky;
oblivious of the clouds around them,
stopping to pause on clear blue heaven;
egg-laying or preening or whatever it is
that gets them rubbing their little legs together.
Probably something thoroughly unpleasant
now I come to think of it. But who am I to judge?
I've stomped on a few blue skies in my time,
strutted my stuff and struck some silly poses,
generally unaware of the wonder around me.
Occasionally, of course, I lost it altogether,
buzzed and crashed and ended up wasted,
upside down on a windowsill somewhere,
legs waving frantically in several directions.
They've gone quiet now. The light has changed.
The combe has darkened except for a patch
of tearaway sunlight, charging over the down.
It's moving across the pasture, the brooding firs,
making the larch-buds blush vermillion
and the spindly ash stand out bony white.
There's a spring coming, beyond that a summer.
Maybe this year I'll stop and take notice.

Spring Rhythm

Turned a corner, saw Magnolia, folded-over sugar-pinkness, bright against the brittle blue. Saw Quince, saw brick-red blossom Quince, standing bashful by a wall. Saw Witch hazel, saw Cyclamen, saw Daisy, beaming like kids with a secret.

Heard Jay, heard Finch, heard Robin and Wren, heard Blackbird chortling like a winner at the bookies, heard Moorhen with her wittering chicks.

Then I heard Swan beat the sky like a drum, and I followed her rhythm and came to the heart of it, and seeing became hearing and hearing became feeling and I knew what I felt and at last I said, *Yes!*

A Little Bit of Grit in the Machine

Just now I saw two magpies chasing a squirrel;
the little squirrel leaping for its life, the magpies
strangely quiet, determined.
                                 I thought how cruel
these primitives were and fell to wondering
if that was why old gamekeepers used to string
them up on gibbets in the woods. I remembered
being scared by their lifeless turning, their slow
iridescence and their fly-blown eyes.
                                     I clapped
my hands angrily, and shouted till the magpies
peeled away. Then I sat back and listened to the
morning, content to be the instrument of some
near-natural justice. Presently the exiled squirrel
returned – and started raiding birds' nests again.

Rough Ground near Huntsham

Miles away by now,
the stag has moved on,
magnificent shoulders
rippling indignantly,
caked in Devon clay.
The ground here is torn,
raked where he antlered it,
ripped at the bracken
in high hormonal rage.
The hedge-bank too
is rutted and pitted,
hooves trampling through
to the arena beyond,
the field where he paced
in parallel and prepared,
judged and gauged
the moment of challenge,
ultimately fought the interloper,
fought till bone and spirit
could take no more
and he lost everything:
tribe and territory,
position and pride,
lost all reason for being here.
At night you can hear him,
by the edge of the moor,
belling his challenge
to a disinterested world.

Mount Pleasant

Alone that morning, in a field of thistles and ragwort,
she was overtaken by a mist of sadness that swept
up out of the secretive combes below Eggardon.

He was blissfully unaware, having woken to the croak
of a raven on the pine behind them. *Look! Listen!*
There he is again. Aren't they supposed to be messengers?

She stood downhill from him, watching the landscape,
with its greys and greens, its weight and solemnity,
while a bird of prey keened from a high blue loneliness.

She remembered the night they made love in the open;
how she had looked up and embraced the stars,
assured for the first time of her place amongst them.

She recalled how she'd started putting a name to things:
water-mint, hogweed and rosebay willow herb.
Now, when the hawk cried, she knew it was a buzzard.

Hold me, she called at last. *Come here and hold me.*
So he went to her, cheerful at first, then concerned,
worried that he might have somehow failed her.

I never knew till now, she said. *It was just another word.*
And as she spoke the tears began to well.
Nature was something you drove through to get to places.

The Shepherd

Talking easy with John Moore, shepherd.
Sixty-odd and slow but quick to grin;
simple-wise in the way of men who work
and love and stay with a piece of land.

Been on the Hill for thirty-three year now,
he says looking down at his sheep-greasy cap.
Been up to London. I couldn't stand it.
Been married. She left. Been in love. She died.

He's worked his way through so many winters
you'd expect him to be hard as a thorn.
Something has softened him though,
made him gentle, kindly, far-eyed and tender.
He would say he'd been saved by the work.

John doesn't sleep much, too many dreams.
At lambing time he doesn't sleep at all.
Nineteen nights in the fold last February,
just him left awake with the ewes and the stars.
At harvest he'll be working after eleven,
the lights of his tractor burning off the night.

He's the kind of man it's good to be around,
talking about the weather or the price of lambs.
How a Swaledale cross makes a Dorset uppish,
prone to jump fences and get itself hurt.

I love it here, he says at last. *I do love the quiet.*
As he speaks a buzzard wheels above us,
inspecting the pasture with a ruthless eye.
Well then, says John Moore, as if to the buzzard.
And he grins – turns – goes back to the work.

V

THE PORTABLE OASIS

A Doodle at the Edge

Another meeting, another agenda, another
list of buzz-words, initials and initiatives.
PSU is entering Phase Three
while the CDR wants G2 to go to Level Five.

If we go the full nine yards on this one;
if we get pro-active, get out of the box, get
our teams together and on the same hymn-sheet;
if we hit the ground running, if we downsize HR,
if we get the money onboard, and our asses into gear,
then we can change something, make a difference,
change what the other guys changed last week.

Meanwhile the god has left the garden,
the muse lies minimised in the corner of our screens.
Not dead, not buried, but ignored and unseen,
like a doodle at the edge of an action plan.

Me? I say make a sacrifice to the doodle;
pick some flowers, speak a poem, feed the tiny muse.
Draw, paint, sing or dance, and you'll bring the gods
back into the board room; the laughing, smiling,
weeping gods of the night-time and the wild.

Immortal

He tore round the corner,
judging it to the millimetre:
full-on, busy, impatient, and young;
expensive hair cut, well-pressed suit,
blue shirt with just a hint of red in the tie.
I expected him to look clean through me
but he stopped, dead in his inside tracks –
like a prince in a myth at a crossroads or a bridge,
when he meets the one-eyed, wizened dwarf.
We stood, each waiting for the other to speak,
strangers, yet not unknown to each other.
It was as if he wanted something, and I had it to give.
The hunger in him was palpable; the hunger
of a man who needs some solitude, or a drink,
or a friend, or a damned good cry. We waited
as his hand gripped and re-gripped his briefcase,
knuckles whitening as he made a fist,
then relaxed, then made it again more tightly.
Finally, I broke the spell, said, *Can I help you?*
No! he said and stepped around me. *No!*
and briskly walked away.

               I watched him go,
watched the suit diminish, and cursed myself
for a fool. I shouldn't have said the 'H' word,
you see. I shouldn't have offered him help.
When I was like that, when I was immortal,
I couldn't have borne a kindness.

The Idea

Even the coffee tastes good today.
Hunched over tables, leaning in,
excitement building in a rising circle –
excited looks, excited gestures,
grunts of approval, exclamations.
That's it... Like that... Spot on... Exactly...
We've been working on that one too...
Laughter now, layered with delight,
connection colliding with coincidence,
synapses snapping to amazed attention,
everything informing the one idea.
And somewhere out there, a shapeless notion,
waiting to be noticed, to be landed, pulled in –
the missing piece, the vital ingredient,
the essential component, Factor X.
In its own time it comes, arising naturally,
named just the once or merely inferred,
gathering itself with implosive momentum,
like demolition footage run in reverse:
a cloud of rubble unsettling itself,
bricks flying in from all directions,
forming, rising out of dusty chaos,
towering, complete and wholly new.
Then, the silence, the precious moment,
the circle of sparkling, enlivened eyes,
the unspoken praise in every smile,
the collective sigh that says, *This is it.*

Between Dream and Action

And who betrayed you?
Who rose up darkly between dream and action
to comfort and stab with equal aplomb?

Did you see the signs?
Did you read the language, of eyebrow and shoulder,
of significant look and dismissive wave,
the unwitting giveaway in a shrug or a sneer,
the dull, lizard eyes behind a smile?

Or was it you who betrayed yourself
with your restless hunger and second-hand certainties?
Maybe you were ambushed by your need to be loved,
or your seeping-cynical view of the world?

What betrays us is the insistent past
which demands that we play out its family fugue –
statement, restatement, in endless repetition,
parlaying a wound into a way of life.

The past, we can be sure, plays both major and minor.
We may not choose to notice, but it's always there.

The Chosen One

They give you precisely one hour, over lunch.
They control themselves. They give nothing away.
They know just how long to spend on each topic:
how long to sound wistful about holidays or golf,
and exactly when to offer you the bejewelled
dagger of duplicity.
              They place it, gingerly,
on the linen cloth, between the bread and the salt,
where it catches the light as the talk moves on,
to your progress and future within the organisation.

Doing what they want means risking everything,
because everything said will be unattributable.
You know it. They know it. Everybody knows it.
Everybody knows you'll be on your own.
                     Coffee,
and the dagger is nudged an inch towards you.
Nothing is said, but while they sign for the bill,
you are expected to pick up the dagger; to say
yes to the deed, like an acolyte of the Assassins,
like the chosen one whose time has come to move
out into the darkness.
               In the fifty-ninth minute
they have to dash. Their parting handshake is firm
and brisk, their eyes are clear and full of meaning.
You stay on afterwards, in the empty restaurant,
staring at the blade and the jewel-encrusted handle.
You ponder fine notions like integrity and loyalty
but they mean nothing when weighed against words
like mortgage, and family, and the kids' education.
When you reach out your hand – as you know
you must – you notice you're no longer shaking.

On Waking Suddenly

Something there and not there. Something
hovering between sleeping and waking,
an atavistic memory perhaps or something
imagined, an old, half-digested dread,
resurfacing like marsh-gas rising in a pond,
a bubble, breaking the surface to drift awhile
until – pop – nothing, nothing at all except
a faint but lingering stench, a hint of something
other, dark and vegetal, fermenting far below.
Just that and the pattering rat of fear.

Career Moves

No, not an evil man. A man of compromise, perhaps,
a man who wandered from the narrow fenland track,
who lost himself among the rushes and was grateful
for the sound of bullish voices just beyond the sedge.
An ambitious man, certainly, and glad to see the light
that floats like Jack o' Lantern just above the mire.
This was how he fell, for Shiny Jack is what you want
and he had always wanted power as much as money.
He made his choices and, little by little, he followed,
until the path was lost to sight and he was drowning.
By increments he had become the very thing he hated.
Reflected in a stagnant pool he saw his father's face.

Do what I say, boy. You're under my roof.

Why have a dog and bark yourself.

They don't have to like me.

It's respect that matters.

You got a problem?

You want one?

Just do it.

Now.

A Culture of Change

You smile the old smile
as you offer him a seat
but those times together
when you were young,
those innocent times,
mean nothing now.
It's a business decision.
You'll keep to the facts.

Your wives are the friends
if the truth were known.
Men make up the numbers.
And this one was always
a bit of a wimp, unless you
were standing beside him.
A business decision, then.
Best to keep to the facts.

He's stunned, of course.
You have to tell him
at least three times.
He doesn't seem to hear.
We do things differently.
You simply have to go.
It's a business decision.
Let's stick to the facts.

And typically he blows it.
He starts to whine. He begs.
You're appalled, repelled,
disgusted, angry. You're glad
you made a business decision,
glad you stuck to the facts.

A Change of Culture

Everything happens very quickly.
The job, the car, the friends, the dream,
all vanish overnight.
Suddenly you're going down the pipe,
a nobody with nothing,
and nothing to look forward to.

You become a social security number,
shuffling shoes in an endless queue,
a little bag of memories, spilled out
in vain across a pawnbroker's mat,
sifted, sorted, priced and rejected.
You learn to lie – they expect you to.

One of us becomes one of them,
a transparent man with an arrogant step,
a jaunty smile and a haunted look,
the type you used to follow like a sniper,
picking them off with distant pity.
You learn to hate – selectively.

And then one evening, by the river,
your pockets stuffed with final demands,
you look at the skyline and see a sunset
so finely washed you catch your breath.
Sensing a delicate change in the seasons
you savour the world, and you are opened.
You wander home, trembling and amazed,
exalting in a sudden awareness.
You kiss your wife as if for the first time
and later that night you wait up,
watching over her. When the tears come
at last, they feel wholesome and clean.

The Interview

I need the job, Jimmy said, looking down
as the Manager smiled his capable smile –
taking in the shoes and the triple shave,
the effort that took the edge off the shabbiness.

Do you know anyone who works here, Jim?
Can you give me a personal reference...?

Danny, he said, remembering a friendship,
the times they'd shared and the beers after work,
the pact they'd made as ambitious young lions,
to shake the world and watch each other's backs.

Okay, said the Manager. *We'll get back to you.*
and he floated away with a handshake and a smile,
wafted on a scent of good new cloth and money.

It was months before Jimmy found out about it
before the Manager wrote... apologies...
no vacancy... not suitable... overqualified...

Later the two bumped into each other. Jimmy
was working but the Manager had been ousted,
sacked to make way for their mutual friend.

D'you know why I didn't give you that job?
said the Manager nursing his one-drink-too-many.
Your friend, Danny. Said you couldn't hack it.

On Being an Englishman and Having a Nice Day

An American woman calls me at the crack of dawn.
She wants me to know how disorganised I am.
I already know this but she needs to tell me anyway.
She says, *You're disorganised.* I say, *Yes.* She says,
I've never known such a disorganised organisation.
I don't say anything much but I think three things:
firstly, she's right; and secondly, she's never lived;
thirdly, I think this woman's beginning to piss me off.
I don't feel anything, except that I note a small shift
inside me, like a tiny ember tumbling in a grate.
Then, as she continues to pass me under the harrow
I close down. I go numb. The blood leaves my skin,
my hands go cold and, as her voice moves up another
octave, I find myself wondering what it would be like
to put my hands around her throat and strangle her.
She's getting into her stride now, and so am I.
As she itemises my failings, one by one, I get her
down on the floor and throttle her, along with
my mother, and a gaggle of would-be-mother clones.
Finally she stops and says something American about
making this a 'learning experience' which comes
across in English as, 'Let that be a lesson to you,
my man'. I wipe the tell-tale spittle from my mouth
and whisper, *Thank you, madam. Have a nice day.*

The Heroes of Everyday Life

No great discoveries, no leaping eureka moments,
no vast overarching schemes or achievements,
but the daily rituals of getting on –
the school-run, the gym, the drive to the office;
a kind word here, some friction there,
maybe some rivalry, a hint of an edge;
queuing for lunch and counting the calories,
shop-talk that eats up the precious hour;
meetings and calls, the occasional trip –
the promise of adventure, the sniff of romance,
though home as usual with presents and a sigh
to the midnight tenderness of kissing sleeping heads.
These are the heroes of everyday life,
neither visionary nor driven, but reliable, steady,
with curbed desires and attainable goals:
the house, the holiday, the golf club, the car;
the yearnings, the hungers, and the ache for a purpose.
They're our friends and acquaintances, husbands and wives.
They are parents, consumers, the pillars of the world.
They are the audience. They are the led.
What do we know of their silent sacrifices?
What can we know of their spiked, unspoken dreams?

The Contract

A word from the led

And in the end we follow them –
not because we are paid,
not because we might see some advantage,
not because of the things they have accomplished,
not even because of the dreams they dream,
but simply because of who they are:
the man, the woman, the leader, the boss,
standing up there when the wave hits the rock,
passing out faith and confidence like life jackets,
knowing the currents, holding the doubts,
imagining the delights and terrors of every landfall;
captain, pirate, and parent by turns,
the bearer of our countless hopes and expectations.
We give them our trust. We give them our effort.
What we ask in return is that they stay true.

Cathedral

Morning is stirring out in the suburbs
while, down at Headquarters, the building rises:
cleaned, dressed, polished and immaculate,
corporate marble awaiting the click
of well-heeled, focussed decision makers.
The atrium creates a dynamic hush
of awed expectation, hope and ambition.
Elevators stretch and limber up,
their mirrors, veneers and ascendant buttons
shining in honour of reason and results.
Above, the chantries and clerestories
of reception, corridor and meeting room
already hum to the whirr of machines,
conversing with others a half a world away;
tapping out the plainsong, the murmuring data,
the call and response of order and action.
Higher still, at the top of the tower,
in a sleek, teak-lined, cloud-carpeted cell,
in the holy-of-holies where things are blessed
or cursed, confirmed or cast out,
there is a silence, a flat uncertain silence,
the silence of exhaustion, anxiety, doubt.

Suits

Suits collect in corners. Preening themselves,
they congregate in navy worsted groups
to practise competition and their golf-swing.

Suits are strong on imperfections. They know
that others' failings, pointed out, can only show
they are themselves a cut above the rest.

Suits in mode like sudden shears, rip and slash,
instinctively feeling out each others' weaknesses.
When it comes to friendship, suits make sacrifices.

Suits triumphant, sit in buttock-clenching fear,
designing neat revenges, hounds-tooth ploys
to serve out those they've striped and checked.

Suits, when pressed, admit to loneliness. Racked
at night by intimations that their lives, their plans,
their very dreams are meaningless and hollow.

Sifting the Silence

Say a little prayer for the friends you've lost;
the ones who shied away from friendship,
calling you weak for being kind,
and the ones you pushed away yourself,
playing the hero in a movie called *'The Job'*.

A hero has few enough buddies at thirty.
Work kills trust and sometimes kills a friend.
The roaring pack of endless youth
becomes a thoughtful, mortal band,
decimated by failure and fear in competition.

At thirty-five you're down to ones and twos.
You tell yourselves the prize is worth it
and ignore the signs that say 'Beware'.
You get your head down, redouble your efforts,
and soon you're entering heart-attack country.

You turn up, shocked, at a couple of funerals
and then you're forty, and alone.
That's when you start spilling your guts out,
pissed, in pubs, to disinterested strangers
or in bed to women who quickly grow tired
of carrying yet another man's pain.

Your body is tense. You long to be held
but nobody touches you because you're in charge.
So you sit in your office, sifting the silence,
and sometimes at night you think about calling
one of the fellas who fell off the wire.

E-mail from the Soul
For Richard Olivier

Somewhere downtown in the busy world,
amongst the siren-haunted high-rise,
there is a place or a time where something
tremendous is waiting to happen.
In a moment the over-carpeted world can change;
the walls you learned to lean against can give,
swing wide, to reveal a hidden landscape
of unimaginable promise – right there
amid the plans and the projected targets.

It is the call: the call that makes the MD quit,
that gets the Head of Systems into chaos.
It's a fax from the past, an e-mail
from the soul, an internal memo
from the psyche, or from God.
Sometimes it comes in a single, headline flash
but more often than not it's in the detail,
the niggling detail that becomes a voice
that says, *I must change. I must change my life.*

And when it sounds – so clear and so terrible –
you're frozen with the fear of it.
Matthew sits dumbstruck, staring at his money,
afraid of the messenger with his prayerful hands.
And Paul, before that business trip to Damascus,
ignoring the voices in the ink and the olives;
Paul, the coldest of them all, driven to the point
where only blinding could make him stop;
even Paul, who changed the world, was afraid
and trembled because he knew the truth –
that in the end the call demands love.

One Last Silver Stair

When I have climbed this one last silver stair,
I shall seek out the half-forgotten places
At the gentle beating heart of the wood.
And sitting there I'll summon up the faces,
The vile, the hard, the broken and the good.
And we shall bathe our aching spirits there,
When I have climbed this one last silver stair.

The Winner

To succeed, he checked-out years ago,
went missing – like you do.
Grabbed a couple of comforting notions,
packed some prejudices and did a runner.
Left his body – like you do.

Filled the hole with coffee and smokes,
a few drinks at lunchtime – like you do.
Then later a few between six and the close.
There's nowhere to go and you daren't go home.
Best to get high again – like you do.

Left his body but the ache remained.
Tried to work around it – like you do.
Tried to explain when she threatened to leave.
Threatened her back, said he'd fight to the end.
Waved as she drove away – like you do.

Saw that he'd lost himself years ago.
Tried to get sorted – like you do.
Cleaned himself up and got back into action
but the trap-door opened and he fell through.
That's when he hung himself – like you do.

St Michael's, Up Marden

A drowsy downland morning
surrounds the dirt-poor church
and twenty generations of prayer,
hurt, despair and thanksgiving
are reduced to a single, agitated fly
whirring above the shabby pews.
I have been here before, been
bathed in this silence, baffled
by its willingness to accept me
in all my foolish disguises.
I have felt the weight of comfort
urging me to surrender, to sit
as others have sat before me;
their chalk-muddied boots
on the uneven brick floor,
their hearts full to bursting
with the relentless hymn of life.
Once I even felt the immanence
of something – in this Christian
place let us call it God,
though the ground here was holy
long before Christ – something
that welled from the very stillness,
that held me and soothed me
like a fractious child.
                         I wasn't ready
back then. I had to go away,
to break and to be broken, to feel
the teeth in things... But now
my impulse is to weep, to grieve
for the years that I have lost,
like a busy yet distracted fly,
buzzing through a vast tranquillity.

The Bones of the World

I have a fondness for rounded stones.
I'm taken by their secrets, their characters
and their patience. I'm a collector.
I've a room full of them, arranged on plates,
in bowls, placed individually, just so,
or together in groups on the wooden floor.
I built a Japanese stone garden once,
before my plans got the better of me,
a shade-garden, filled with ferns and moss.
It centred on five great lowering boulders,
and granite pebbles that glowed
when they were wet. I tended it for years:
a city-boy samurai, placing each stone
with the fullest attention; relishing the cool
on summer evenings and the way the rocks
seemed to change with the seasons;
now serious, now melancholy, now pulsing
with energy. I was proud. I lost them all.
Later, when I traced the line of my past,
I took to picking up stones on walks;
weighing myself down with flints and fossils,
adding to the cairn of my petrified griefs.
They say that circles are a sign of healing
and that rounded stones are a kind of mandala.
I don't know much about signs and symbols
but I do know that every pebble spoke to me,
that each one beckoned, and that one by one
they drew me in – some with their beauty,
others with their calm – and that finally
they led me back to the world of people
and things, where they were seen as nothing
more than doorstops and paperweights.

Slack Tide

I am standing at the jetty again,
where the marsh water meets the unkind sea.
I've dreamt this light at the end of the day,
the reddening of the pines and the gilded shingle.
I've heard the sounds of the fishermen on the water
and the low rhythmic creak, the dip and the plash,
as the ferryman rows his way towards me.
I can see him clearly, head to one side,
narrow back towards me as he reaches forward,
digging at the water with the heavy oars,
pulling through easily in spite of his age.
He's studying me now through rheumy eyes,
expression half-buried in a rounded shoulder.
I want to wade into the water and pull him ashore.
I want to say, *Look, I kept my promises,*
but we both know of promises I have yet to keep.
It's not such a terrible thing to fail,
to feel the loss of a hundred petty luxuries.
It's harder by far to let the dreaming go, and
the need to be loved for the next achievement.
For years I was nothing but my plans.
And all the while the ferryman was here,
achieving no more than another crossing;
building nothing, just coming and going,
bending himself to the tide and the weather.
He hasn't changed from the man of memory;
his watery eyes still spill their kindness,
and his spotted hands still grip the oars
as if they've grown right out of the wood.
There's a comforting bump of oak upon oak
and a sudden smell of iodine and creosote.
The ferryman throws me a length of painter,
climbs onto the jetty, and looks me in the eye.
She's yours now, he says, and walks away.

In My Fiftieth Year

October had me thinking about dying.
The specialist had dropped a few new words
into my humdrum, day-to-day vocabulary,
sharp, angular words like prostate, blood test and tumour.
I waited as the days grew shorter, burned faster,
turning for consolation to Alden Nowlan and Raymond Carver,
poets who both died conscious at fifty,
facing the implacable mugger that is cancer.

Alden got there by main strength and character,
eyeball to eyeball with the merciless thug,
managing to raise a modicum of grace
at each new threat and ugly demand.
Ray was something else. He'd made the journey,
had travelled to despair and way beyond.
He knew that his life, or what he had left of it,
was a gift over which he had neither right nor dominion.
In fact he renounced all pretence to control
and settled for the astonishing beauty of the moment.

Having seen the mugger's shadow in the alleyway,
having heard the click of his approaching heels,
I've seen him, in his irrational way
move on, seeking someone else to terrorise.
Whatever comes now, I think I'm ready.
My life, like Carver's, has become a boon.
For me, each day's an unexpected benison,
a deepening I never thought to witness.
I'm privileged to see beauty and to know what I'm seeing,
to recognise love in its glory and variety.
I have a place where my heart can gather itself,
I have friends, and the goodwill of my dead.
In my fiftieth year I have come in to land.
Rich in love and beauty I am truly blessed.

Acknowledgements

Speaking for Cinna was commissioned by Shakespeare's Globe to be spoken on the 400th anniversary of the first production of Julius Caesar, September 1999; *A Poem that Speaks for Itself* was written in connection with programmes delivered for The Praxis Centre, Cranfield University, School of Management, 2001; *The Heroes of Everyday Life* and *Between Dream and Action* were written for the 5th Arts & Business Conference, Castle Borl, Slovenia, July 2002; *The Contract* was written during a short residency for the Work Foundation and Ashridge at the Ashridge International Leadership Conference, August 2002; *Anyone Can Sing* was written during a Mandorla, Rites of Passage retreat for men at Cae Mabon, May 2002.

Other acknowledgements are due to: The Office for Public Management, The Core Trust, The Dulwich Poetry Competition Anthology, Psychopoetica and Poetry Monthly.